Guide to
STOCKHOLM

Text: Judith Sampognaro

Photographs: Nils-Ingvar Svensson and Magnus Svensson,
Cindor; with the co-operation of Erik Nyberg (pp. 2-3 and cover),
Nationalmuseum (p. 9), Chad Ehler (pp. 21 and 67),
Karl-Erik Granath (p. 23-a), Ola Österling (p. 26),
Moderna Museet (pp. 33 and 34-a), Hans Ekestang (p. 34-b),
Hans Hammarskiöld (pp. 51 and 52-a), Jurek Holtzer (p. 54-a),
Marie Andersson (p. 53), Owe Svensson (p. 78-b),
Alexis Daflos (pp. 77, 83-a and 84), Ulf Hjert (p. 85-b),
Lars Holter/Eddie Granlund (pp. 81-b and 82).

Design, lay-out and printing, entirely created
by the technical department of
EDITORIAL FISA ESCUDO DE ORO, S.A.

© EDITORIAL FISA ESCUDO DE ORO, S.A.
www.eoro.com

© CINDOR
Box 1103 - 18311 Täby (Sweden)
Tel: 08/792 42 52 - Fax: 08/792 42 51

Aerial view of Stockholm.

THE VISIT TO STOCKHOLM

Stockholm, built on some fourteen islands joined one to another by bridges, is one of the most beautiful cities in Europe. Seen under the blissful effects of the northern light, the Swedish capital has all the appearance of a floating city. Bathed in golden sunlight, the high towers of the Riddarholm and German churches, the cathedral and the Town Hall stand out clearly against the blue sky. The waters of the Baltic Sea wend their way to the very heart of the city in the east, whilst those of Lake Mälaren lap against the western banks. The lake forms a great rectangle, bordered by the islands of Söder, Kungsholmen, Riddarholmen and Gamla Stan, its waters finding their mouth at Strömmen on the Baltic Sea at a point marked by a strong current in the middle of the city, famous for its salmon fishing. Lake Mälaren being above sea-level, shipping has to pass through locks –Slussen in the southern part of the city centre, and Hammarby in Orstaviken. Vessels of all sizes, moored in the city's docks, form part of the very physiognomy of Stockholm.

The principal buildings rising over the city centre include the Royal Palace, the Parliament and, a little further off, the Town Hall. Towards the outskirts of the city, along the Mälaren, stand the bridges carrying traffic through Västerbron and Essingen. The city is bounded by its former customs posts –Skanstull in the south and Norrtull and Roslagstull in the north– and which mark the border between the city centre and Greater Stockholm. The new zones of the city grew up like so many floral crowns beyond the old customs posts, each characterised by the town planning style prevailing at the time of their construction. The city centre, a veritable treasure-trove of tourist attractions, is small enough to be visited on foot, whilst the different sights in the outskirts can be reached by public transport and boat services. The beauty of the city, its natural environment, combining bodies of open water and tree-filled parks, provide visitors with infinite possibilities for recreation. The museums of the city, many of them of international standing, the concert halls and theatres, the Stockholm Opera House and the Cullberg ballet are just a few of the many, many attractions offered to visitors.

View of Lake Mälaren.

HISTORICAL BACKGROUND

The lands which now make up the Kingdom of Sweden were still covered by ice in the year 11000 BC, and it was another 6,500 years before the Baltic Sea and the Scandinavian countries acquired a geographic extension similar to the present. The first chronicles mentioning Scandinavia date to the early Christian period and describe the region as a country inhabited by many tribes, each with its own chief or king. Two of the most powerful of these peoples were the Goths in Götaland and the Svears in Uppland. The latter gave their name to Sweden, as Sverige (the Swedish name of the country) means Kingdom of the Svears.

Viking expansion began in the 6th century, bringing the Scandinavians into contact with other lands and cultures. The first known record of their sea raids was the sacking of Lindisfarne Abbey in northeast England in the year 793. The Swedish Vikings, unlike the Danes and the Norwegians, were attracted eastwards, their expeditions reaching the Black Sea and the Caspian Sea and establishing trade links with Byzantium and the Arab empires.

The first Viking trading town, Birka, located on an island in Lake Mälaren, attracted many foreign traders. Ansgar, the first Christian missionary, landed in Birka in 830 and was allowed to preach and found a church, but failed to win many over to the faith in a country where pagan gods were venerated. The principal of these was Woden or Odin, the All-Father and king of the gods. Beside him stood Thor, the god of Thunder and of Strength, and Frigga, goddess of Fertility.

The pagan cults fell into disuse in the 12th century, but left their lasting mark on the art and literature of the region.

The first ruler of all Sweden was King Olof Skötkonung. Olof was the founder in the 10th century of the first medieval city, Sigtuna, whose creation caused the decline of Birka. After his reign, however, his descendants were unable to retain power, and the struggle between different families for the throne started up once more. During the Middle Ages, Baltic trade was dominated by the Germanic cities of the north, grouped under the Hanseatic League. The swift development of agriculture and trade led to the establishment of new cities, populated at first by traders and craftsmen of German origin. During his reign, Birger Jarl, who established the Folkung dynasty in 1250, began the conquest of Finland, fostered the growth of the Hanseatic League in Swedish cities and founded the city of Stockholm. The Nordic countries, then, formed a community of shared interests, even though they vied with one another for control of the region. The economic crisis of the late Middle Ages exacerbated the power struggle in Sweden, which culminated in 1397 with the signing of the Kalmar Union: Margaret, queen of Denmark and Norway, received the Swedish crown, thus uniting the three Nordic countries under a single monarch, as Finland was already under Swedish domination. When Eric of Pomerania, Margaret's cousin, was made king, he tried to break with his country's economic dependence on the Hanseatic League. This affected foreign trade and led to the imposition of new taxes, fomenting widespread popular discontent. In 1434, the peasants and min-

View of Skeppsbron avenue.

Lake Mälaren and the islands of Riddarholmen, Gamla Stan and Skeppsholmen.

ers of Dalarna, led by Engelbrekt, rose up against Eric. Engelbrekt was later assassinated and the Sture family took over the regency. Four years later, Sten Sture the Younger deposed the Archbishop of Sweden. As a result, the Papal Court excommunicated him and Christian II of Denmark found the excuse he was seeking to invade Sweden.

In 1520, after two failed attempts to take Stockholm, Christian won a decisive battle in which Sten Sture met his death. Stockholm then surrendered, and Christian II was crowned king of Sweden in Stockholm Cathedral. In 1521, the peasants and miners of Dalarna rose up once more, led by Gustav Vasa, and the Danes were finally expelled. Gustav

View of the city in the 18th century.

Vasa was crowned as King Gustav I in 1523 and during his regency the bases for the Swedish state were established.

The hereditary monarchy was restored and Sweden was converted to the Protestant religion. The expropriation of church goods helped to fill the coffers of the state and after his death his children maintained the power of the dynasty for over one hundred years.

With the rise to the throne of Gustav II Adolf in 1611, Swedish expansion began, reaching the Russian border to the east and annexing Estonia and Livonia (Latvia). Gustav II Adolf led his country into the Thirty Years War, his successes making him a powerful presence in Europe. On his death, his daughter, Kristina, heir to the throne, was just six years of age. Chancellor Oxenstierna was made regent, and continued Gustav II Adolf's policies, achieving Swedish domination of the Baltic. When Kristina took over the throne in 1644, she brought all the most brilliant minds of the day to her court. After her conversion to Catholicism in 1654 she abdicated, spending the rest of her life outside Sweden.

During the late-17th century, the throne was occupied by Karl XII, who spent his reign engaged in military campaigns beyond the Swedish borders. His initial successes finally ended in defeat at Poltava in 1709 and loss of control of the Baltic.

A new political age was brought in with the 18th century, when parliamentary power was strengthened. The country also enjoyed a period of economic, cultural and scientific development at this time. The war with Russia in 1741 resulted in the defeat of the Swedish army and, finally, the loss of Finland heralded in a time of political instability which culminated in 1772 with Gustav III's coup d'etat.

Under Gustav III, all areas of Swedish cultural life flourished, as this enlightened despot protected the arts and founded important cultural institutions. However, the domestic political situation was highly unstable throughout his reign: the nobility was unhappy with the loss of its political power, and Gustav was finally assassinated in 1792. With the disappearance of this last link with the Vasa dynasty, the Swedish parliament designated the French Marshall Jean Charles Bernadotte heir to the crown. Taking on the name of Karl Johan, the new king surprised all and sundry by forging an alliance with Russia and Prussia against Napoleon and establishing a union with Norway which was maintained until 1905. After that time Sweden, enjoyed a long period of peace during which the power of the monarchy was only slighter greater at present. The present king, Karl Gustav XVI of the Bernadotte dynasty, is a constitutional monarch who exercises purely protocolary functions.

Statue of King Gustav Vasa by Carl Milles (Nordic Museum).

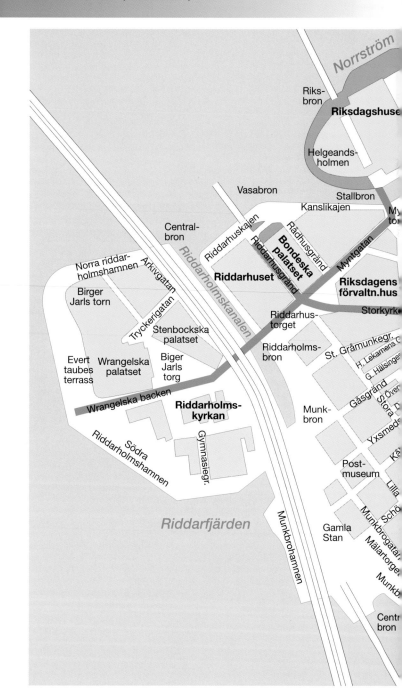

Stortorget square

1. GAMLA STAN (Old Town)

A tour of the old town (Gamla Stan) forms the core of any visit to Stockholm. Built on the islands of Stadsholmen, Riddarholmen and Helgeandsholmen in the 13th century, Gamla Stan grew up around the fortress of Tre Kronor, where the Royal Palace now stands, and was surrounded by a great wall. Two roads, Västerlånggatan and Österlånggatan, later absorbed into the urban fabric, had their starting-point here. As we shall see, many of the streets of Gamla Stan still conserve their old medieval air.

In the heart of the old town is **Stortorget Square**, a bustling place of trade and gatherings in medieval times. Here stood the original town hall building, as well as the prison and the stocks where offenders were punished. In olden days, the inhabitants of Stockholm would come to this square to draw water, to trade, to jeer at the miscreants condemned to the stocks or merely to amuse themselves for a while. The square was also the scene of an important historical event, known as the "Stockholm blood bath", when Kristian II of Denmark was being crowned in the cathedral and the ceremony was brusquely interrupted by the execution of nearly one hundred people for political reasons. The severed heads of these unfortunates were left to roll around the muddy ground of the square for three days, staining even the surrounding streets with blood. Less dramatic is the tradition, going back to the 16th century, of installing a Christmas fair in the square each year for the sale of arts and crafts, Christmas

Börshuset (former Stock Exchange).

decorations, food and sweets, a tradition maintained even until today. Three important streets have their origin in Stortorget Square: Köpmangatan, Svartmangatan and Skomakargatan, all of them lined by elegant 17th- and 18th-century Germanic-style buildings. On one corner of the square, dominating the whole, stands the **Börshuset (former Stock Exchange)**, a pale-coloured palace in the neo-classical and rococo styles. This is the work of Erik Palmstedt, King Gustav III's favourite architect. It was built on the site of the old town hall and officially opened in 1776 by the king himself. The Stockholm Stock Exchange occupies the ground floor, whilst the upper floor is the seat of the Swedish Royal Academy, whose members annually select the winner of the Nobel Prize for Literature.

Two other buildings also stand out in Stortorget Square: Grillska huset and Schantzska huset. **Grillska huset**, at number 3, on the corner with Köpmansgatan, conserves its original medieval structure, though it has been altered on several occasions since its construction. The side fronts of the building are in the baroque style. Grillska huset, which is now owned by the charity organisation Stadsmissionen, houses a cake shop and, at number 5, a small church.

The cake shop is renowned for making the most delicious fairy cakes in the entire city. For its part, at number 20, on the corner with Kåkbrinken, **Schantzska huset** is a typical 17th-century palace, decorated by a leading sculptor of the period, the residence of rich merchants and high officials at the Swedish court.

From Stortorget, we take Trångsund to Storkyrkobrinken. In this

The Järnpojken statuette.

street, at number 2, we find the palace known as the **Oxenstierna palatset**, which dates from the second half of the 17th century. Red in colour and adorned with sandstone decorations, the palace is built in the Italian Renaissance style. Although unfinished, Oxenstierna palatset is considered one of the architect Jean de la Vallée' finest masterpieces.

Returning along Trångsund, we pass in front of the cathedral (Storkyrkan), but before entering will visit Slottsbacken. Here, on the right, at number 2, is the **Finnish Church**, or **Finska Kyrkan**. Originally, there were two houses here where people came to play pelota, until the church was installed in the smaller of the two in 1725. The larger building, where Gustav III's first opera house was installed, was demolished in 1792. Behind the

Buildings in Gamla Stan.

Skeppsbron avenue.

church building, which dates from the mid-17th century, is a tiny garden containing the smallest statuette in Stockholm, the **Järnpojken**. This is a sculpture of a seated child, beloved of locals and visitors alike, who lavish special care on him. In winter, he is always warmly wrapped up in a red woollen hat and scarf.

Next, at Slottsbacken number 4, we come to the **Tessinska palatset**, built as the residence of Nikodemus Tessin the Younger, the architect who designed the Royal Palace. Famous for its tiny garden, this building is now the official residence of the civil governor. We now continue to walk along **Slottsbacken**, which means "the descent from the castle" and was, in the Middle Ages, a sand and gravel path separating Tre Kronor Castle, the centre of power, from the medieval city. At the end of this descent, on the right, is **Skeppsbron**, an avenue running parallel to the lake. Skeppsbron was designed during the so-called Age of Greatness in the 17th century, to reflect the importance of Stockholm. Powerful merchants moved their offices and homes to the new avenue, and great ships from all over the world moored at its docks. This was also where the financial barons of the time, known sneeringly as the "Nobility of Skeppsbron", became established. One of the most outstanding buildings on Skeppsbron is at number 28, where the German merchant Johan Martin Schön of Lübeck lived, having bought and joined the two houses which stood here in 1768, installing his offices on the ground floor. This rich trader was also known for his elegant attire, and was always dressed in the most fashionable suits, with silk stockings and one of his collection of four wigs, which allowed him to vary his hairstyle. He completed his attire with an imposing gold walking stick. The building was owned by the Schön family until 1917, when it was sold.

We now go back up the rise to the **Storkyrkan (Stockholm Cathedral)**. Its original Gothic front was demolished in the first half of the 18th century and replaced by one in the baroque style. Built in honour of Saint Nicholas, the cathedral is first mentioned in a document dating to the year 1279. After the Reformation, Gustav Vasa confiscated most objects of value in the building. Inside, on the south wall, is a painting, Vädersolstavlan, representing Stockholm one April

View of the cathedral.

Sculpture of Saint George and the Dragon in Köpmanbrinken, a bronze replica of the original produced by Bernt Notke for the cathedral.

day in 1535. This is the oldest painting conserved in the city. In the northeast section of the cathedral is an oakwood sculpture entitled Sankt Göran och draken (Saint George and the Dragon), by Bernt Notke of Lübeck. This work, which took six years to complete, was installed in the cathedral on New Year's Eve 1489. Visitors can watch the changing of the Palace guard from the top of the cathedral tower, which also commands magnificent views over Stockholm.

Leaving the cathedral, we take the street on the left, **Prästgatan**, which encircles practically the entire island until, at the corner with **Kåkbrinken rise**, we find the remains of a rune stone (a stone inscribed with ancient Scandinavian writing) embedded in the wall of a building here. The stone was probably found nearby and used as construction material. According to the inscription, the rune stone was erected by a couple, Torsten and Frögunn, in honour of their son.

We now take a street parallel to Kåkbrinken, Västerlånggatan, turning into Kindstugatan at Tyska brinken to reach the **Tyska Kyrkan (German Church)**, a magnificent construction dating from the 17th century. The streets around the church are lovely open spaces, a pure delight to stroll around.

Taking Västerlånggatan once more, we come to **Mårten Trotzigs gränd**, the steepest and narrowest little street in the entire city, with 39 steps and a width of just 90 centimetres, so that if we stretch out

Mårten Trotzigs gränd, the narrowest street in the capital.

our arms we can touch both sides at once. The street is named after a rich German trader, once the owner of several of the buildings along it.

We now head for the **Järntorget (Iron Garden)**, once a busy trade centre where iron was weighed and inspected for export, an open space perfect for the work of the stevedores who loaded goods onto the waiting ships. There were many taverns in this area, where the seamen came to eat and drink, as well as many brothels.

Österlånggatan and Västerlånggatan.

Taverns and restaurants formerly abounded in the old city. During the reign of Queen Kristina, when Stockholm had a population of around 30,000, there were some 200 taverns selling beer and liquor, not to mention the drink sold by wineries and small eating-houses. When, years later, trade and seafaring activity moved to Skeppsbron, the square was converted into a financial centre, enjoying a new period of splendour after the establishment of the first national bank in 1680.

The Royal Palace.

Near the square on the corner of Österlånggatan and Tullgränd, is the **Gyldene Freden restaurant**. This legendary eating-house is linked with the national poet Mikael Bellman, whose ballads masterfully sketched out life in the streets and taverns of old Stockholm. The restaurant, traditional meeting-place of Swedish intellectuals, was bought in 1920 by the painter Anders Zorn, who later donated it to the Swedish Academy, which uses income from it to finance the Bellman literary prize. The front of the building features an 18th-century sign representing an angel holding the dove of peace in his hand in an allusion to the peace signed in 1721 and which marked the end of two decades of war.

At Järntorget, Västerlånggatan meets Österlånggatan, a quieter street with fewer shops and businesses leading to the **Kungliga Slottet (Royal Palace)**. The present building dates from the early-18th century, when it was erected over the ruins of the palace of Tre Kronor (Three Crowns), destroyed by fire in 1695. The Royal Palace was built according to plans drawn up by the architect Nikodemus Tessin the Younger and combines the Italian Renaissance and baroque styles. With a rectangular ground plan, the building is organised around a large inner courtyard and also has an outer courtyard where the traditional changing of the guard takes place. There are 608 rooms, all magnificently decorated with tapestries, paintings, fine furniture and other adornments. The most outstanding rooms in the Royal Palace include: the Throne Room (with engraved silver throne dat-

Royal Palace: crown jewels.

The Changing of the Guard at the Royal Palace.

View of Riddarholmen and Riddarholmskyrkan.

ing to 1640); the Treasure Room (where the Crown Jewels are kept); the Bernadotte Gallery (featuring portraits of the royal family); the Apartments of King Oskar II (in rococo style): and the Queen Lovisa Ulrika Rooms (with a magnificent collection of Italian painting). The palace church, with its excellent acoustics, is another architectural jewel, built by Carl Hårleman according to a drawing by Nikodemus Tessin the Younger.

The **Slottsmuseum (Palace Museum)** features an exhibition of the different phases in the construction of the building itself, whilst the **Gustav III Antikmuseum**, housed in the north wing, contains objects acquired by King Gustav III, a great lover of art and archaeology.

Though Drottingholm Palace, in the outskirts of the city, is the present residence of the royal family, the Swedish monarchs continue

Wrangelska palaset.

to have their offices in the Royal Palace, as well as using some of its rooms for official ceremonies and gala dinners. Guests are also accommodated at the Royal Palace whilst on official visits.

Our next port of call is **Riddarholmen**, whose name, "Knights' Island", alludes to the palaces which noblemen and knights built here in the 17th century. This peaceful, silent island, where there are no shops, commands magnificent views of Riddarfjärden, Södermalm and Kungsholmen. In the 13th century a monastery was founded here by Franciscan monks, who also began to build a church which later served as the base for the **Riddarholmskyrkan (Church of Knights' Island)**. The church is now a museum where most of the Swedish monarchs are buried. The needle-shaped iron tower was installed to replace an earlier one made of copper which was destroyed by fire in 1835.

Nearby is **Wrangelska palaset,** the royal family's residence for many years after the fire at Tre Kronor Palace. It was here that King Gustav III was born. The palace now serves as the seat of the Appeals Court. Beside it stands Birger Jarls torn, a lookout tower built in 1530 using bricks from the old Klara Monastery in Norrmalm. At the top of the pillar is a statue of Birger Jarl, the founder of the city, by Fobelberg in 1854.

We now cross the bridge to visit the **Riddarhuset (Knights' House)**, a magnificent example of the baroque architecture of the Period of Grandeur. This was where the Swedish nobility used to meet, and the many rooms in the palace are adorned with nearly

Riddarhuset (The House of the Nobility).

two thousand noble emblems of the most important families in the country.

Finally, crossing the Stallbron bridge, we reach the tiny island of **Helgeandsholmen**, dominated by two buildings dating to the late-19th century: the **Riksdagshuset (Parliament)** and, adjoining it, the **Riksbank (National Bank)**. And this is where our first route around the city of Stockholm ends.

Helgeandsholmen: the Riksdagshuset (House of Parliament).

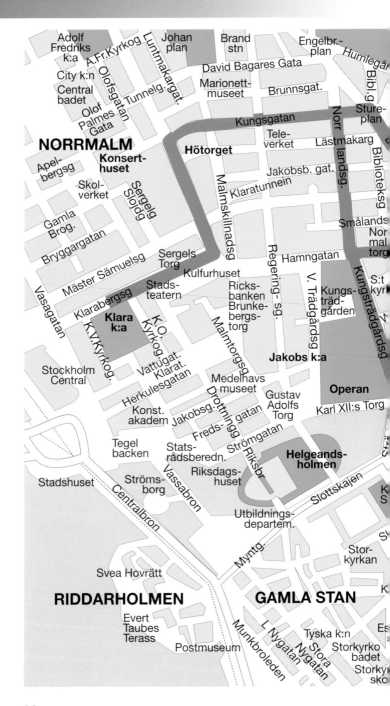

Gustav Adolf square.

2. SKEPPSHOLMEN – THE CITY

This second route takes us around two areas of Stockholm. The first of these, to the east of the Old Town on the other side of the Strömmen current, includes Blasieholmen and two islands, Skeppsholmen and Kastellholmen, joined by a bridge. The second is a central area of shops, offices and museums in the Norrmalm district, known as the City.

Our starting-point is **Gustav Adolfs torg**, one of the busiest squares in the whole of Stockholm. At one end stands the **Kungliga Operan (Royal Opera House),** built in the late-19th century according to plans drawn up by the architect Anderberg and which includes the theatre itself and the **Operakällaren**, a neo-baroque restaurant dating to the same period. At the other end of Gustav Adolfs torg is the **Arvfurstens palats**, with a façade dating to the 18th century, now the seat of the Ministry of Foreign Affairs, whilst also of interest is the **Medelhavsmuseet (Mediterranean Museum)**, housed in a 19th-century building on the corner with Fredsgatan street and devoted to exhibitions on the ancient civilisations of the Mediterranean region. In the centre of the square is the **statue of Gustav II Adolf**, the work of Pierre Hubert Larchevéque in 1796.

We now take Strömgatan street to **Blasieholmen,** where great palaces were built in the 17th century to which were added many luxurious buildings in the 19th. One of the most renowned of these is the **Grand Hotel**, a French-style construction built by the

Royal Opera House.

architect Axel Kumlien in 1874 and whose original front has since been altered considerably. Dating to the same period is the building which adjoins the Grand Hotel, the **Bolinderska**, at number 6. The construction of this edifice was commissioned by two leading industrialists, Jean Bolinder and L. O. Smith. The sumptuous interior decoration has now been restored.

Nearby is the **Nationalmuseum (National Museum)**, the second

Boats to Vaxholm and other islands in the Archipelago depart from the Blasieholmen dock, between the Grand Hotel and the National Museum. In the background on the left, Chapman's sailing ship.

The National Museum from Skeppsholmen, and a painting by Carl Larsson.

most important official building here since the construction of the Royal Palace. It was designed in Renaissance style by the German architect Anibal Stüler and inaugurated in 1866. Its principal collections centre on art from the 15th to the 19th century, with a section devoted to such 19th-century Swedish painters as Carl Larsson, Zorn and Liljefors. The inner entrance to the building features a mural by Carl Larsson.

Crossing Skeppsholmsbron bridge, built over 130 years ago, we come to the island of **Skeppsholmen**, known as the "museum island", though its name really means "boat island". Skeppsholmen and the island next to it, **Kastellholmen**, form a tiny oasis in the middle of the city and command magnificent views of Stockholm. The beautiful tree-filled park on the two islands was created in the late-18th century on land occupied the previous century by naval bases. The **Amiralitetshuset (Admiralty House)**, which stands near the bridge, was built in the mid-17th century as the navy secretariat and was later altered by the architect Fredrik Blom, who nonetheless conserved the original entrance. In fact, nearly all the buildings on both islands have a military past, even the **Skeppsholmskyrkan (Skeppsholmen Church)**, which was the admiralty parish church. When the fleet was transferred to Muskö in the late-1960s, cultural institutions and museums began to be established on Skeppsholmen, converting the island into a cultural centre. Skeppsholmen is also well-known for **Chapman's sailing ship**, a sailing boat anchored at its docks and now converted into a much-loved youth hostel.

Further on, we come to the **Arkitekturmuseet (Swedish Museum of Architecture)**, which shares its entrance with the **Moderna Museet (Museum of Modern Art)**, designed by the Spanish architect Rafael Moneo and containing important collections of 20th-century art. Here are represented all the best-known names in contemporary art in a collection of 4,000 works, around half of

Museum of Modern Art.

A painting by Otto G. Carlsund (Museum of Modern Art).

them by Swedish artists. The building, which stands beside the original museum premises, is a work of art in itself.

Behind the Moderna Museet is the **Östasiatiska museet (Museum of Far Eastern Art)**, housed in an 18th-century building designed by the architect Tessin the Younger and converted into a museum in the 1960s. The museum boasts the largest collection of Asian art in Europe, with sculpture, painting, ceramics and other objects embracing a large period from the Stone Age to the late-19th century.

From here, we return to the city centre, passing through Karls XII square to **Jakobs torg**. This tiny square is lined on all sides by fine

Kungsträdgården metro station.

Kungsträdgården: statue of King Karl XII, the rear façade of the Opera House and St. Jacobskyrka church.

buildings, including the late-Gothic **Jacobskyrka (the Church of Saint James)**, built in honour of the Apostle James in the mid-17th century. There is also a private palace in Jakobs torg, Makalös, built in the first half of the 17th century. According to legend, the owner of the palace, Jacob de la Gardie, went out into the street one day to admire his mansion, the most beautiful palace in Stockholm. This display of vanity awoke the wrath of God, who condemned him to blindness. De la Gardie, repenting of his sin, donated money to embellish the nearby Church of Saint James (Jacobs Kyrka), thanks to which the tower was built.

The entrances to **Kungsträdgården Metro station** are in Rege-ringsgatan and Arsenalsgatan streets. This is one of the most attractive stations in the city's underground system, decorated by the artist Ulrik Samuelsson. The decor represents an underground garden, with waterfalls and plants, and an archaeological exca-vation site, with copies of remains from the Makalös palace. The Stockholm metro or underground, almost half of its one hundred or so stations beautifully decorated, has been called the longest art gallery in the world. Many artists took part in the work, mak-ing their personal contributions to its diversity of styles and dec-orative elements and motifs.

Kungsträdgården (King's Garden) is a lively meeting-place

View of Kungsgatan with the two Royal Towers (Kungstornen).

throughout the year. In winter, there is skating here, whilst in summer the cafés and restaurants put out tables under the limes. King's Garden is particularly busy at night. A skating rink is installed around the **Statue of King Karl XII**, by Erik Göthe, and a full programme of entertainment is organised here in summer. Passing on, we come to sculptor Petter Molin's famous **fountain**, sculpted in plaster in 1866 and later cast in iron. The fountain represents the meeting of the Baltic with the Mälaren. Kungsträdgården was once the king's private garden, hence its name. Nonetheless, all it conserves from those times are the tree-lined avenues on either side, as the garden was completely destroyed in the 19th century.

On the corner of Hamngatan street is the **Sverigehuset (Sweden House)**, a tourist information centre, whilst a little further on we find the exclusive **Nordiska Kompaniet (NK)**, the first department store in Sweden, designed in 1915 by the architect Ferdinand Boberg, who took the ideal of the great American stores as his inspiration.

Still on Hamngatan, just before we get to Nybroplan, is the private museum of **Hallwylska palatset**, housed in one of the last great palaces to be built in Stockholm, in the late-19th century.

This was the residence of the Countess Hallwyl, who inherited one of the largest fortunes of the period. The house is conserved just as it was when the countess died, and remains to give testimony to the splendour of a by-gone age. The countess's old Mercedes parked in the garage, the bottles of wine in the cellar, her collection of porcelain and personal effects all remain intact. The Countess Hallwyl, an obsessive collector, spent her days documenting even the smallest items in her peculiar collection and on her death left an enormous register made up of 78 tomes.

Opposite the palace is **Berzelii park**, the oldest in the city, where Berns Salonger, a restaurant which has conserved its reputation for excellence over the passing of time, first opened its doors in 1863. We shall now explore **Kungsgatan street**, which joins the eastern and western parts of the Norrmalm district, better known as The City, now an area full of shops and cinemas. The two towers we see on either side of the street, known as the **Kungstornen (King's Towers)**, date from 1926 and were, in their day, the highest skyscrapers in Europe.

The **Konserthuset (Concert House)** stands at the corner of Sveavägen and Kungsgatan. This is a blue building, typical of Swedish architecture in the 1920s. Besides concerts, this palace is also the venue for the Nobel Prize award ceremony each year. The main entrance, with its steps, gives onto Hötorget square, facing a fountain representing Orpheus by Carl Milles (1936).

Konserhuset (Concert Hall).

Hötorget.

Hötorget ("Hay Square") was used as stables in the times of King Gustav Vasa and as a store by peasants, who kept hay and straw for animal fodder here. The plan for the modernisation of the city, carried out in the 1950s and 60s, began with the zone between Hötorget and Sergels torg and environs, Firstly, the old Hötorget was demolished, followed, one by one, by the buildings in the adjoining blocks, where five skyscrapers were built in their place, along with large shops, offices and banks. Nowadays, Hötorget is a market-place filled every day by flower, fruit and vegetable stalls.

Admirers of the Swedish actress Greta Garbo should now make a short detour to the **Pub department store** in Drottningatan street, as a small museum devoted to the movie star, who worked in the shop as a young girl, has been installed in the basement.

Taking **Sveavägen avenue**, we can now make another detour to visit two places of interest. The nearer of the two is on the corner with Tunnelgatan, where the Swedish prime minister Olof Palme was assassinated in 1986. A plaque indicates the exact spot where this tragic event took place. The tomb of Olof Palme is in the cemetery of **Adolf Fredriks**, a church which stands just short way off, with a gravestone exemplifying the simplicity typical of the Swedish. The second place of interest, which we come to by taking Tegnérgatan and then turning left into Drottningatan, is **Blå Tornet**, the house where the novelist and playwright August Strindberg spent the last years of his life and which has now been converted into a museum.

Back in Hötorget square, we now take **Sergelgatan**, a busy shopping street named after the well-known mid-18th century Swedish sculptor Sergel, and where he once had his studio. At the end of the street is **Sergelstorg** square and the **Kulturhuset (House of Culture)**, recognisable for its peculiar glass column, 38 metres high. Sergeltorg is a hive of bustling human activity, as well as a popular meeting-point. For its part, the House of Culture offers exhibition rooms, theatres, a library, cafés and restaurants as well as, on the ground floor, Designtorget, a sales point for Swedish arts and crafts and design.

We now continue our walk by taking Klarabergsgatan to the side entrance of the **Klara Kyrka** church, before which stands a statue of the Swedish poet Nils Ferlin, one of the best-known of the intellectuals who frequented the Klara district, with its print-shops, newspapers and cafés in the 1930s and 40s. The oldest parts of the church date to the late-16th century, though the building has since been altered on several occasions. Inside, the angels over the altar are the work of the sculptor Sergel. In the cemetery is the tomb of national poet Carl Michael Bellman. In the Middle Ages, this was the site of a convent which Gustav Vasa ordered destroyed in 1527 and of which no trace now remains.

Sergelstorg.

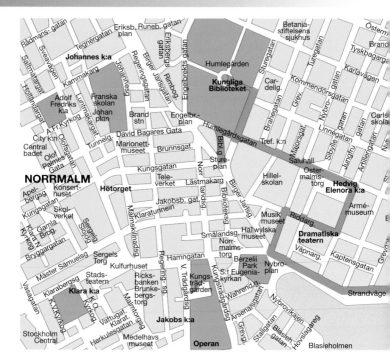

3. ÖSTERMALM - GÄRDET

This entire zone had a distinctly rural character for many years, when it was occupied by grazing animals and cattle barns. The area became known as Östermalm in around 1885, when a radical process of transformation converted it into the upper class residential quarter we see today. The old houses and shacks were demolished and the land flattened with dynamite to make way for straight, wide streets in accordance with the ideal of the period. The avenues of Strandvägen, Karlavägen and Valhallavägen, great new promenades, were built in this way, gracing the perimeter of the new urban area. Östermalm is also where many cultural and educational institutions have their headquarters, such as the Technical University, the Music Academy and the Film Institute, most of them situated around Valhallavägen avenue, as well as many museums. To the north of Valhallavägen lies the Gärdet district, built in 1930, and where the functionalist style has clearly left its mark.

We begin our tour of this area in **Stureplan**, a central square which is well known due to the peculiar concrete "mushroom" which offers shelter from rain. This great plaza was formerly an important point of interconnection for the city tram service, and is still a popular

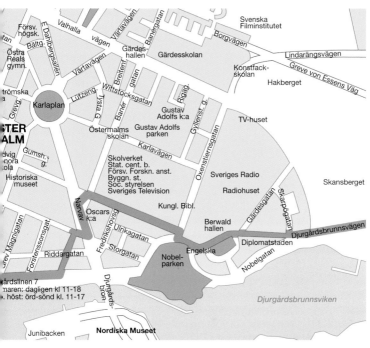

Svenska
Filminstitutet

Borgvägen

Försv.
högsk.

Valhalla
vägen

Gärdes-
hallen   Gärdesskolan

Lindarängsvägen

Östra
Reals
gymn.

Konstfack-
skolan

Greve von Essens Väg

Hakberget

Karlaplan

Gustav
Adolfs k:a

TV-huset

Östermalms
skolan

Gustav Adolfs
parken

Karlavägen

Skolverket
Stat. cent. b.
Försv. Forskn. anst.
Byggn. st.
Soc. styrelsen
Sveriges Television

Sveriges Radio

Radiohuset

Skansberget

Historiska
museet

Kungl. Bibl.

Oscars
k:a

Ulrikagatan

Berwald
hallen

Diplomatstaden

Djurgårdsbrunnsvägen

Riddargatan

Storgatan

Nobel-
parken

Engelska

Nobelgatan

gårdslinen 7
naren: dagligen kl 11-18
. höst: örd-sönd kl. 11-17

Djurgårdsbrunnsviken

Junibacken   **Nordiska Museet**

Stureplan.

meeting-place. On the right of the square is the **Sturegallerian** shopping gallery and an old bath-house, the **Sturebadet**, which first opened its doors in 1885, originally in the building now occupied by the gallery. After the Sturebadet burnt down in 1985, it was decided to rebuild the baths according to the original plans, with the addition

Royal Library.

beside them a shopping gallery of international status. The late-19th century exteriors were combined with modern interior design elements, using such materials as marble, granite and fine woods, including ebony and cedar. Once finished, the site won an important international design award.

Near the square is the **Humlegården** park, whose name alludes to the fact that hops (humle) were once grown here to make beer for the Royal Palace. Inside this great park is the **Kungliga Biblioteket (Royal Library)**, which contains a copy of everything published in Sweden and whose original collections were made up of books belonging to Queen Kristina and works rescued from the fire at Tre Kronor palace. The library was built between 1871 and 1878, but was later extended to accommodate the thousands and thousands of books and manuscripts which line its burgeoning shelves.

Leaving the park by the north gate, in Karlavägen avenue, we approach **Lärkstaden,** a district whose name means "city of larks" (the popular name for prostitutes) in an allusion to the fact that this was once a red-light area. The district, one of the prettiest in the entire city, lying between Odengatan, Valhallavägen and Engelbrektsgatan, contains many houses of original architectural style, such as those in Danderydsgatan street, which are painted in pastel colours and sport tiny gardens. In the centre of Lärkastaden, on a hill, stands the **Engelbrektskyrkan** church, in Art Deco style and formed by several bodies with roofs at different heights over which rises the high tower. The church was inaugurated in 1914.

Engelbrektskyrkan church.

We now return to Humlegården park where, on the right, stretches the Östermalm quarter with its tall, palatial buildings, those nearest the gardens most worthy of our attention. Here, in the area bounded by Nybrogatan, Humlegårdsgatan and Grev Turegatan, are count-less shops and restaurants. Taking one of these thoroughfares, Humle-gårdsgatan, we reach **Östermalmstorg** square, at one end of which stands **Saluhall**, the prettiest market in the city, housed in a red brick building with an entrance of medieval appearance. Over recent years, many restaurants and small cafés have also been established on the market premises. Another side of the square is occupied by the baroque **Hedvig Eleonora kyrka**, a church with a beautiful copper dome designed by the architect Jean de la Vallée in the mid-18th century.

Behind the church, at Riddargatan 13, is the **Armémuseum (Royal Army Museum)**, replete with collections forming a review of the wars in which Sweden has been involved. Closed for seven years, it was newly opened in spring 2000, its rooms completely reno-vated and reorganised in line with a new concept of the muse-um, focused now on military activity in civil society and everyday life. Full-scale figures dressed in period uniform, their factions modelled in latex, give an extra touch of realism to the different sections.

In nearby Sibyllegatan street, at number 2, is the entrance to the **Musikmuseum (Music Museum)**, which boasts a collection of some 6,000 instruments and features reconstructions of musical scenes

Östermalmtorg and the Saluhall market, with a view of the interior.

from different historical periods. The museum is housed in an old industrial building, built between 1580 and 1720, used originally to bake bread for the army.

We now continue along Sibyllegatan to **Nybroplan**, where we find the **Dramatiska Teatern (Dramatic Theatre)**, a simple Art Deco building with a white marble front inaugurated in 1908. The theatre, which has several different stages, was decorated by leading artists of the time and features particularly the paintings in the interior by Prince Eugen and Carl Larsson. The top of the façade is adorned by sculptures by Carl Milles representing the different expressive

Royal Army Museum.

forms of art –Poetry, Drama, Sculpture and Painting– whilst the lower part features a relief by Christian Erikson representing Dionysus. The Dramatiska Teatern is renowned for its productions of classical and modern plays, and Ingmar Bergman has directed many of the great universal plays here.

Strandvägen, a broad avenue lined with magnificent buildings which runs parallel to the Nybroviken harbour, has its origin in Nybroplan.

The Drama Theatre, in Nybroplan.

In the late-19th century, Strandvägen became the preferred place of residence of the richest families in Stockholm, who commissioned the most famous architects of the day to design their mansions. Amongst these, most outstanding is that at numbers 29-33, Bünsowska huset, built in 1880 for a rich timber merchant according to plans drawn up by the architect Isak Gustav Clason, who also designed the Nordic Museum building. **Bünsowska huset** is composed of three buildings sharing a common façade. Also of interest is the house at number 35, built in 1890, which boasts an entranceway rich in carved adornments.

Strandvägen.

History Museum.

At the end of Strandvägen we turn into Narvavägen avenue to visit the **Historiska museet (History Museum)**, which is devoted to the prehistoric and Viking periods and to the Middle Ages. The most interesting of its sections, displaying pieces of incalculable value, is the so-called Gold Room, opened to the public in 1994. Here we can admire, amongst other items, unique works from the 5th and 6th centuries, including necklaces, bracelets, pendants and medallions.

Further to the east, on Djurgårdsbrunnsvägen avenue, are several more fascinating museums: the **Sjöhistoriska museet (Museum of Maritime History),** with collections devoted to sea trade and naval defence, the **Telemuseet (Telecommunications Museum)**, whose exhibitions relate to the history of technology and industry in Sweden); and the **Folkens Museum Etnografiska (Ethnographic Folk Museum)**.

Near these museums is the **Kaknästornet**, a 155-metre high communications tower built in 1967 by the architects Bengt Lindroos and Hans Borgström. The tower also houses an information centre, souvenir shop and restaurant with panoramic views over the city.

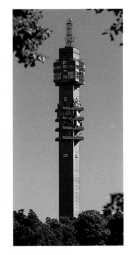

Kaknästornet.

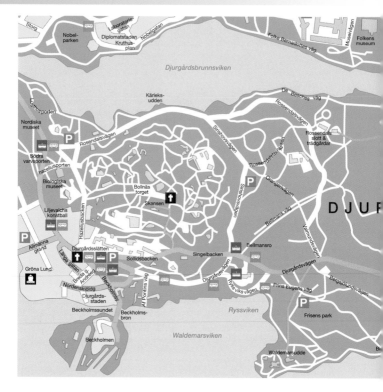

4. DJURGÅRDEN

The name Djurgården alludes to the royal hunting grounds which King Johan III ordered built in the 1570s and which were converted into an attractive recreation ground for the inhabitants of Stockholm in the 18th century. We can enter this great park from Strandvägen an ornate bridge, the **Djurgårdsbron**, opened in 1897, or using the boat service which takes passengers from Nybroplan to different points on the island and on to the Slussen dock in Gamla Stan and the old city. A tramline also has its origin in Norrmalmtorg, adjoining Nybroplan, going along Strandvägen avenue before entering Djurgården, where it stops at all the principal points of interest.

Crossing the Djurgårdsbron bridge, we see on our right, like a fairy-tale castle, the **Nordiska Museet (Nordic Museum)**, devoted to Nordic popular culture and the Swedish way of life and work over the course of history. The museum, which occupies a building constructed in the late-19th century according to plans drawn up by the architect Isak Gustav Clason and one of the

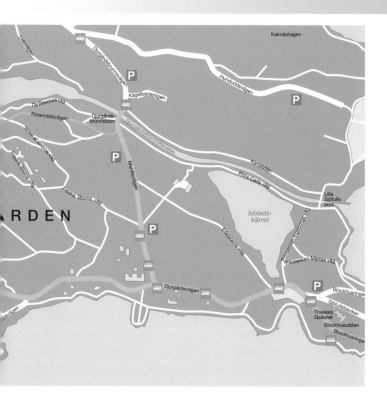

Nordic Museum.

Junibacken: Pippi Långstrump (Pippi Longstocking) is one of the most popular characters created by the Swedish writer Astrid Lindgren.

most outstanding monuments in Stockholm, was founded by Arthur Hazelius, a Swedish ethnologist who also set up the Skansen open-air museum, described below.

Behind the Nordic Museum is **Junibacken**, a space devoted to children's culture and whose central themes are taken from the stories of the Swedish writer Astrid Lindgren. One of the principal attractions here is the Sagotåget story train, which takes passengers on a tour of the places invented by the author in her tales.

Not far off, in **Vasamuseet,** is the museum devoted to famous galleon the Vasa, 68 metres in length, which sank on its maiden

The Vasa Museum.

The Royal galleon, the Vasa.

voyage in 1628, shortly after being launched for the first time, due to its excessive weight and disproportionate height. The Vasa was raised from the seabed 300 years later and brought from Skeppsholmen to the docks of the Galärvarvet shipyard. The name of this shipyard refers to the type of warships, known as "galär-er", which used to moor here in the winter months. Thousands of objects and pieces of wreckage from the sunken vessel were also found during the operation to raise it, and it was the work of years to put this jigsaw together. The galleon had to be continuously sprayed for 20 years with a curtain of water containing a special substance in order to conserve it. The Vasa has had its own museum since 1990, occupying a building organised to allow visitors to view the vessel from all angles.

The Vasa was the largest ship ever built in Sweden and was to have demonstrated the power and supremacy of King Gustav Vasa in the Baltic. Despite its initial failure, the Vasa is now a success, as it is one of the most popular tourist attractions in Stockholm.

Detail of the stern of the Vasa.

We now continue our route along Djurgårdsvägen avenue, almost immediately reaching the **Biologiska museet (Biology Museum)**, with its exhibition, in natural conditions, of a complete representation of Nordic animal life.

A little further one, we come to the **Aquaria vattenmuseum (Aquaria Water Museum)**, which contains different Nordic and tropical aquatic environments, aquariums with sharks and other fish, corals, and waterfalls with salmon and trout.

Adjoining the Water Museum is the **Liljevalchs konsthall (Liljevalchs Art Gallery)**, one of the loveliest art centres in Northern Europe, where exhibitions on Swedish, Nordic and international art past and present are organised.

The next point of interest on our route is the hundred-year-old **Gröna Lund funfair** which, besides offering many typical fairground attractions, is also a venue for open-air concerts. Like the Vasamuseet, we can also reach Gröna Lund directly on the ferry from the Slussen dock in Gamla Stan near Nybroplan. The short voyage is made all the more memorable by the beautiful views of the city passengers can enjoy from the boat.

The Gröna Lund funfair.

Skansen: farm.

Back on Djurgårdsvägen avenue once more, passing the Djur-gårdskyrkan church, we come to a typical neighbourhood of wooden houses which began to be built in the 17th century: **Djurgårdsstaden**. Breda gatan and Långa gatan streets, their houses adorned with oil-painted wooden panels, are particularly picturesque and well-conserved.

From Djurgårdsstaden we can take the bridge leading to the tiny island of **Beckholmen**, which was for many years a military zone closed to the civil population. At the highest point on this island stands **Stenvillan**, built in 1835 by the architect Fredrik Blom. This mansion, with a neo-antique front, is now a private house, but was once used by the wholesale traders' association.

We now return to Djurgårdsvägen avenue to visit **Skansen**, the oldest open-air museum in the world. In 1891, Arthur Hazelius began his work of documenting the country way of life, under threat of extinction due to industrialisation. His initiative led to the creation of Skansen, a museum which occupies an area of over 300,000 square metres and which provides magnificent testimony to Swedish history. This impressive museum features a large number of faithfully-reconstructed buildings from different periods (houses, farmhouses, granaries, craft workshops, churches, shops, windmills, etc) and typical objects from the different regions of the country. The first buildings installed in Skansen were a house from Darlana and a Lapp camp, and since then the museum has gone on to accumulate over 150 such exhibits. Skansen keeps

Skansen zoo.

historic popular traditions alive, inviting visitors to take part in the festivities held here throughout the year in an atmosphere of times gone by. There is also a zoo in Skansen, mostly for Scandinavian fauna, and the site is also a pleasant place of recreation, with open-air theatres and restaurants.

We now continue to skirt the coast to reach **Waldemarsudde**, a palatial chalet in the Art Deco style now converted into an art gallery. It was built in 1904 by the architect Ferdinand Boberg as the residence and studio of Prince Eugen. Besides being an accomplished painter, the prince was also a keen art collector, and accumulated a magnificent collection of landscapes and portraits which are displayed in the

chalet gallery, which was added later. The kitchen was convert-ed into a cafeteria and exhibitions are held in the attic, where the prince had his studio. In the gardens at Waldemarsudde, which are adorned with sculptures by Carl Milles, Auguste Rodin and Per Hasselberg, stand the oldest and largest oak tree in Stockholm, and a late-18th century oil mill. The site is also renowned for the fine floral arrangements both inside the house and in the gardens.

From Waldemarsudde we now head towards the Thielska gal-leriet museum. The greatest attraction of Djurgården, however, is its scenic beauty, and visitors are recommended to walk along the coast or to hire bicycles to admire the natural splendour of its woods, the coastline and the sea where yachts sail past, cafe-terias housed in old chalets and luxurious mansions such as the **Täcka Udden**. This great house is owned by the Wallenberg fam-ily, one of the most powerful in Sweden, though this did not spare them from the obligation to provide a path along the beach for public use.

Djurgårdsfärja, the ferry communicating Nybroplan with Gamla Stan, which also stops off at the island of Djurgården.

The Djurgårdsbrunns canal.

Leaving Täcka Udden behind us, we reach the **Thielska galleriet**, a white palace with a green dome built for the banker Thiel, one of the richest people in the country and the most important art collector in Sweden in the early-19th century. When Thiel went bankrupt, the local council bought his gallery with its collection of turn-of-the-century works, including paintings by Anders Zorn, Bruno Liljefors, Eugéne Jansson and many more, as well as the largest collection outside Norway of works by Edvard Munch. Since the restoration of the decoration and interiors, the galley has recovered much of its original air, more that of an aristocratic palace than an art museum.

From Thielska Galleriet, we stroll along the coast to **Blockhusudden**, an old customs station at the southern point of the island, built in the 18th century.

We now continue along our route to reach the **Djurgårdsbrunns canal**, which marks the division between the northern and southern parts of the island. Before crossing the Djurgårdsbrunns bridge, however, we can make a detour to the left, along Rosendalsvägen street to visit **Rosendal Castle**, the summer residence of King Karl Johan XIV until his death. The castle still conserves its original decoration and furnishings, all in an excellent state of repair, offering a magnificent glimpse of the lifestyle of the period. Rosendal, which was built between 1823 and 1827 by the architect Fredrik Blom, is also famed for its gardens, where there is a market garden selling organically-grown plants and vegetables and where buyers can pick their own bunches of flowers. The castle grounds, with their ancient trees, majestic amongst pools and gentle hills, are a truly idyllic beauty spot.

A little further on, in **Djurgårdsbrunn**, is a restaurant and picnic area in what is an ideal spot to pause for rest and refreshment. There was a thermal water fountain here in the 18th century, with a bath-house, pharmacy and the restaurant, mostly conserved even today. Boats can be hired on the canal.

The tram which departs from Normalmstorg to take passengers around part of the island of Djurgården.

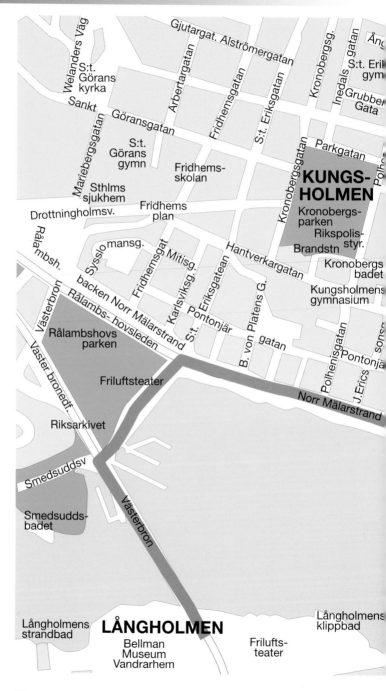

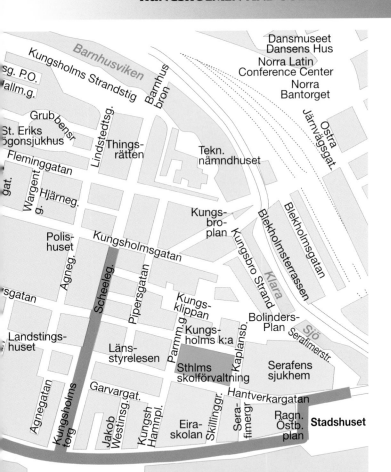

Dansmuseet
Dansens Hus
Norra Latin
Conference Center
Norra
Bantorget

Kungsholms Strandstig

Barnhusviken

sg. P.O.
allm.g.

Grubbensr.

St. Eriks
ögonsjukhus

Lindstedtsg.

Things-
rätten

Barnhus
bron

Flemminggatan

Wargent.
g

Hjärneg.

Tekn.
nämndhuset

Östra
Järnvagsgat.

Kungs-
bro-
plan

Kungsbro Strand

Blekholmsgatan

Blekholmsterrassen

Klara

Polis-
huset

Kungsholmsgatan

Scheeleg.

Pipersgatan

Kungs-
klippan

Agneg.

Parmm.g

Kungs-
holms k:a

Bolinders-
Plan

Kaplansb.

Sjö

Serafimerstr.

sgatan

Landstings-
huset

Läns-
styrelesen

Sthlms
skolförvaltning

Serafens
sjukhem

Agnegatan

Kungsholms
torg

Garvargat.

Jakob
Westinsg.

Kungsh
Hamnpl.

Eira-
skolan

Skillinggr.

Sera-
fimergr.

Hantverkargatan

Ragn.
Östb.
plan

Stadshuset

Riddarfjärden

59

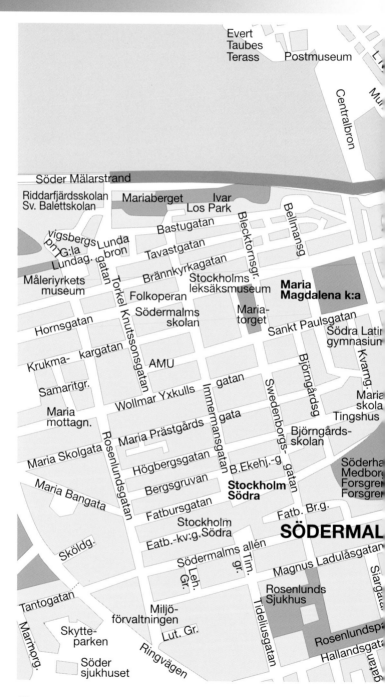

a k:n
Estniska
skolan
SKEPPSHOLMEN
Gröna
Gånger
S.Brobänken

Storkyrko
badet
Generaltullstyrelsen

Nygatan

Storkyrko
skolan

Skepps

den

Strömmen

bergs-
pl.

Katarinav.

Söder-
malms-
torg Slussen
Ryss-
gården

Bussar mot
Nacka,Värmdö

Saltsjöbanans stn.

Katarinavägen

Stadsgårdsleden

Hökens G.
Mose-
backe-
torg gatan

Götgatan

Svartens-

Högberg

Östgötag

Kat.V.Kyrkog

Kat.Ö.
Kyrkog

Katareina k:a

Fjällgatan
Norska kyrkan

SIFU

Stigbergsg

Frans
Schartaus gymn

Tjärhovs-
plan

entars-

Katareina
Västra Skola

Katarina
Norra Skola

Med-
borgar-
platsen

Tjärhovsgatan

Folkungagatan

Nytorgsg.

Borgmästargatan

et
allen
adet

Arbets Kocksgatan
förmedling

Åsögatan

Katolska
Domkyrkan

Söderledstunneln

Åsögatan

Bondegatan

Södermanna-

Medicin
historiska
museet

Renstiernas Gata

Skattehuset

Götgatan

Malmg.v.

Västgöta gatan

Katarina Bangata

Skånegatan

Närkesg

Sofiag.

gatan

Tjust.

Åsö
torget

Åsö
gymnasium

Östgötagatan

Bjurholms
gatan

Brän
nerg.

Katarina Bangata

Kat.s.
skola

Tjurbergsg

Helga- Blekingegatan

Gotlandsgatan

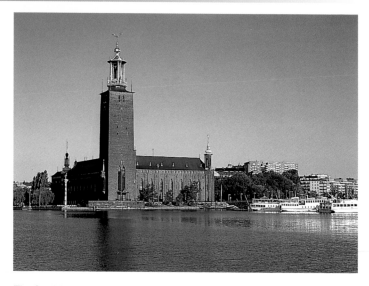

The Stadshuset (Town Hall).

5. KUNGSHOLMEN AND SÖDERMALM

This next route takes us to the islands of Kungsholmen and Södermalm. Far from the centre, near the waterside, Kungsholmen was the ideal location to establish production activities, and the island was first populated by craftsmen and later by industrial workers. Later still, however, the establishments of local administration buildings and the construction of elegant housing along Norr Mälarstrand avenue converted it into an attractive residential area.

Our tour begins with a visit to the **Stadshuset (Town Hall)**, which was designed by the architect Ragnar Östberg and officially opened in 1923. With its large, dark red roof tiles and its tower, crowned by a weathercock sporting the three gold crowns of the national coat of arms, the building reminds us of the Tre Kronor palace in the old city. Visitors can go up the 106-metre-tall tower by lift or by taking the stairs and corridors. Now a symbol of Stockholm, the view from the top of the tower is one of the most beautiful in the entire city, revealing to our gaze the gold domes of buildings, green spaces and soothing waters, a vision enhanced by the famous Northern light, the delight of painters. Every day at twelve noon, the tower carillon, Örjansleken, starts up, the figures of Saint George, the princess and the dragon emerging to the accompaniment of the medieval piece Örjan.

Entering from Hantverkargatan we find, on our right, the famous Blue Room (Blå hallen), where the Nobel dinner and dance takes place each 10 December and, on our left, the Sessions Chamber (Rådssalen). Other fine rooms in the Town Hall are the Prince's Gallery (Prinsens galleri) and, above all, the Gold Room (Gyllene salen), decorated with mosaics of Byzantine inspiration. This lovely building is completed by an outer court-yard with columns joined by arches, and a garden, at whose feet stretches Riddarfjärden Bay.

Leaving the Stadshuset, we take **Norr Mälarstrand**, enjoying a most pleasant promenade. Along the first stretch of this avenue are moored many boats, some of them used as per-manent homes. Heading towards the interior of the island, in Scheelegatan street, is the **Rådhuset**, built in the early-20th century according to plans drawn up by the architect Carl Westman, and now the seat of the law courts.

At the end of Norr Mälarstrand lies **Rålambshovsparken** park, a much-loved spot by the inhabitants of the city, particularly in sum-mer, and an ideal venue for picnics, sport and leisure activities or simply to enjoy a book under the sun's gentle caress. We can also continue along the coast to Smedsuddsvägen from here, to find a beach which is excellent for bathing if the weather permits.

Stockholm Town Hall: the Nobel Prize award ceremony in the Blue Room.

Norr Målarstrand avenue.

From here we can see **Västerbron**, a bridge built between 1930 and 1935 to join the islands of Kungsholmen and Södermalm. Between the two lies **Långholmen**, an island which was given to Stockholm by Queen Kristina. With its parks and wild vegetation, Långholmen is a veritable oasis of peace, a safe haven

Rålambshovsparken.

from workaday life. Leafy willows, the tips of their branches gently stroking the waters, the trilling of birds, the perfume of roses which fills the air, and the idyllic coves of the island, ideal for a refreshing dip on a hot summer's day, combine to form a paradisiacal spot to delight the senses.

A prison stood on this island for 250 years before it was finally closed in 1975, the grimmest of its buildings demolished and the rest converted into a hotel and hostel. Even these, however, help to give an idea of the past rigours of the landscape of this rocky island, bare of all plant life until the 19th century. This landscape contrasts with the beauty and exuberance of the vegetation now found here since, Långholmen lying along one of the accesses to Stockholm from the west, it was decided in the 19th century to improve it. To this end, the prison inmates were given the task of covering the island's rocky surface with earth, after which some three thousand trees were planted.

The **Alstavik** estate, built in 1670, was the site, between 1724 and 1827, of a preventive detention centre for women accused of leading what was considered a libertine life. The building now houses the island's only restaurant. For its part, the **Kronohäktet**, built in the early-19th century, houses the hotel, which promises guests their own key and a fine menu offering rather more than the bread and water diet of years gone by. A cafeteria, open in summer, has been installed in the old

Långholmen.

View of Söder Mälarstrand avenue.

prison courtyard, where the inmates used to take exercise. A small museum on the history of the prison is also open to the public.

We reach Långholmen from **Södermalm** by crossing the Långholmsbron bridge. Beside this bridge, **Söder Mälastrand** avenue, which runs along the entire south side of Lake Riddarfjärden, commands magnificent views of Kungsholmen and its town hall, Riddarholmen and Gamla Stan. At the end of Söder Mälastrand is **Slussen** and Södermalmtorg square, one of the nerve-centres of the island. Though the largest of all the islands on which the city of Stockholm stands, Södermalm still retains the air of a small town. The island's landscape is steep and rocky, with many cliffs, and visitors will find an interesting variety of building types on it.

On Södermalmstorg square is the **Stockholms stadsmuseum (City of Stockholm Museum)**, housed in a fine baroque style building, the work of the architect Niodemus Tessin, completed in 1680.

From this museum, devoted to the city's history, we make for Mosebacke, either on foot or taking the **Katarinahissen** lift, in which case we shall enjoy magnificent views of the city.

Those choosing to walk should take Peter Myndes Rise, Götgatan street and Götgatsbacken Rise. This last is crossed by several small sidestreets –Mariagränd, Klevgränd and Urvädersgränd– which form the remains of the gridwork of medieval streets. At number 3 **Klevgränd** is a tiny house with a yellow front, dating back to the late-16th century and which is probably the oldest stone house in Södermalm. Nearby, at number 3 Urvädersgränd street, in a small 18th-century building, is the **Bellmanmuseet**, a museum devoted to the Swedish national poet, Carl Michael Bellman (1740-1795).

We now continue to Mosebacketorg square, the venue for concerts and other performances since the mid-19th century. The square was urbanised when the Södra teatern was rebuilt in 1859 after being destroyed by fire. It is named after the owner of the mills which stood here in the late-17th century, Moses Israelsson. Fine views of ships sailing for Helsinki and nearby ports can be seen from the **Mosebacke** terrace.

We now take the steps up to Fiskaregatan street and on to Roddargatan. Before reaching the corner of Högbergsgatan and the Katarina kyrka church, we pass through the **Häcklefjäll district**, whose name is linked to a dark period in the history of Södermalm, when it was thought that this was a place where

View from Katarinahissen with City of Stockholm Museum to the left.

witches met. Alleged witches were tried around the Katarina Kyrka in the 1670s and were imprisoned in Södra Stadshuset, now the Stockholm City Museum, to await execution.

On the opposite side of Högbergsgatan stands the **Katarina kyrka** church, with its baroque dome, designed by the royal architect Jean de la Valée in the 17th century. The church, which has been variously altered after suffering damage from fire on two occasions, forms part of those built when Stockholm was becoming an important capital. In the southeast section of the site is the **Sture monument**, erected in memory of the victims of the "Stockholm bloodbath".

We now take a sidestreet, Kapellgränd, to reach the elevation of **Pelarbacken**, Stockholm's oldest place of execution, as well as the last Station of the Cross for religious processions in the Middle Ages. Of the three stones representing the Calvary which were placed here, inscribed with drawings on the life of Jesus, only one has been conserved, and can bee seen in the Medeltids museum in the old city.

Our next stop is **Medborgarplatsen**, a complex containing

Katarina kyrka.

Södertorn and Bofills båge.

meetings rooms, library, cinemas, swimming pool and market, opened in 1939. Not far from this centre is the **Bofills båge (Arch of Bofill)**, a semi-circular housing complex designed by the Spanish architect Ricardo Bofill in 1992, and **Söder torn (South Tower)**, an outstanding example of modern architectural style in Södermalm.

The next point of interest on our route is **number 55 Götgatan** where there was a fashionable drinking house in the 18th century, Källaren Hamburg. This was where condemned criminals where taken for a last drink before their execution. The innkeeper engraved the name of each of these prisoners on their empty glasses, displaying them in a blue cupboard which was later purchased by an American collector. The tradition continued until 1862, when the last execution in Stockholm took place.

From Götgatan, we take Katarina Bangata and then Söder-

Nytorget.

mannagatan, which leads to a tiny square, **Greta Garbos torg**, named in honour of the famous actress, who was born and grew up in this district of the city.

We now take Sofiagatan, soon reaching a pleasant leafy square, **Nytorget**, with open-air cafés on either side of the street.

Picturesque houses in Fjällgatan.

Turning into Nytorgsgatan, we reach **Mäster Mikaels gata**, near the Katarina kyrka. Mäster Mikaels gata street is named after the city executioner, Mikael Reisurer, who lived near here and who –irony of ironies– was himself beheaded as a punishment for killing a wanted criminal when off duty.

At number 6A Mäster Mikaels gata is a 17th-century house and, at number 10, a typical 18th-century dwelling with courtyard, both highly picturesque. Further up, from **Fjällgatan**, we can enjoy splendid views of Stockholm. The surrounding streets, with their 19th-century houses and lampposts, are eloquent of the historic nature of this part of the city. We now go down again, to **Katarinavägen**, an avenue running parallel to the waters of Lake Saltsjön. Here stands the sculpture known as **La Mano ("The Hand")**, by Liz Eriksson, erected in memory of the Swedish volunteers who died in the Spanish Civil War. Finally, in the south of Södermalm, beyond the Skansbron bridge, in Nynäsvägen avenue, is the **Globen stadium**, now a symbol of the city. Built between 1986 and 1989, this is the largest spherical construction in the world, measuring 110 metres in diameter and 85 in interior height, with a volume of 605,000 m^3. This is the venue for events of all kinds, from sports competitions to boating exhibitions and concerts. Beside this impressive structure, a new district has sprung up, with a huge shopping centre, hotels and offices.

The Globen.

Aerial view of Helgeandsholmen and the City Hall.

EXCURSIONS

Stockholm offers practically infinite possibilities for trips and excursions, so much so that, given the sheer size of the city, the visitor may be forced to select just a few of the sights proposed and to leave some of those on the same route for another day. However this may be, we suggest that visitors begin with a visit to one of the most beautiful palaces in the environs of the city, Drottningholm.

Drottningholm

On the banks of Lake Mälaren, west of Stockholm, Drottningholm is the present residence of the royal family, and was the first Swedish monument to be catalogued as World Heritage by UNESCO. Surrounded by a great park reminiscent of the gardens at Versailles, Drottningholm also includes the Chinese Pavilion and a theatre, forming a unique 18th-century palatial site and an outstanding exponent of the European architecture of the period. The palace was built by Nikodemus Tessin the Elder for Queen Hedvig Eleonora, widow of Karl X Gustav, between 1662 and 1700.

This is an excursion with a host of attractions. First and foremost of these is the visit to the palace itself, its rooms conserved intact, and open to the public despite being the private residence of the royal family, and to the baroque gardens, their symmetry and perfection typical of the period when they were built. Here are many fountains and pools, as well as magnificent sculptures brought to Sweden as booty from the Thirty Years War. Another feature of the park is the Chinese Pavilion, testimony to the fascination for things oriental felt by the aristocracy in the 18th century.

The theatre at Drottningholm, the best-conserved of its type in the world and which still has its original decoration and stage machinery, all in perfect working order, enjoyed its period of greatest splendour during the reign of Gustav III, but is still the scene of a popular annual summer season of concerts and opera pro-

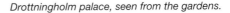

Drottningholm palace, seen from the gardens.

Drottningholm Palace from Lake Mälaren.

ductions. The authenticity of the theatre creates an atmosphere which takes audiences back in time in a truly unforgettable experience.

Visitors can get to Drottningholm by underground to Bromma station and then by bus, or by car from Fridhemsplan in Kungsholmen, taking the Drottningsholmsvägen road. Nonetheless, the most delightful manner of reaching the palace is by taking the Lake Mälaren steam ship to the island of Lovön (departures from the Town Hall docks).

Statue in the grounds of Drottningholm palace.

Birka and Strängnäs

Birka, on the island of Björkö in Lake Mälaren, was the first Viking city in Sweden, its population reaching one thousand. Of the original Viking settlement, no trace remains on the ground, and it is thanks to archaeological excavation that it has been possible to reconstruct part of the past, for tools, remains of buildings and other objects have been unearthed here, illustrating the life of these early inhabitants. Most of these finds are now on display at the History Museum in Stockholm.

Just a few ruins from the old walls which once stretched in the form of an arc around the settlement now remain. Signs and official guides are here to help visitors find the places of interest, testimony to life in the old city, such as the Viking cemetery (with over two thousands tombs), the Ansgar Cross (erected in 1834 at the top of the hill in honour of the first Christian missionary to Sweden), the remains of a fortress, the Chapel of Ansgar (built in 1930) and the Viking Museum.

The island has now been restored to its past natural beauty and vegetation, and Birka now boasts a rich flora whose aroma impregnates the Mälaren breeze in summer. There are no cars on the island, but many tracks and paths allowing the visitor to explore it.

Moreover, Birka can only be reached by sea, on the steam ship which departs from the Town Hall dock.

Birka.

The same boat to Birka can also be taken to visit **Strängnäs**, a beautiful city of narrow streets and 17th- and 18th-century wooden houses. The historic centre, rich in atmosphere, lies at the upper part of the city around the cathedral, whose profile stands out from the heights. This Gothic cathedral was altered on sev-

Strängnäs.

Gripsholm Castle, in Mariefred.

eral occasions between its original construction in the late-13th century and the 15th. Gustav Vasa was elected king of Sweden here in 1523.

Mariefred

Not far south of Strängnäs lies Mariefred, the pearl of the Mälaren, a picturesque city of 18th-century wooden chalets where, a stone's throw from the centre, we find Gripsholm Castle, built by Bo Jonsson Grip in 1370 over the ruins of a medieval fortress. A boat, the Mariefred, takes visitors directly to this lovely town, and is a reproduction of the original vessel which first began to ply this route in 1903 and which was destroyed by fire in the 1970s. It is also possible to reach Mariefred, which lies some 60 kilometres from Stockholm, by car or train.

Skärgården, the Archipelago

Visitors to this area should not miss the opportunity of a trip to the islands. Stockholm is surrounded by some 25,000 of these, forming the Archipelago, a veritable paradise in summer, beloved of the people of Stockholm. Sailing the waters of the Archipelago is a wonderful experience due to the beauty of its fantastic landscape of wooded islands, reefs and islets, open expanses of water and narrow passages between tiny islands. All the islands are different in some way: some have picturesque restaurants, hotels,

Many of the islands in the Archipelago have pebble beaches.

hostels and small shops, whilst others are desert, and the flora and fauna on them is similarly varied.

Summer houses, fishermen's huts, even farms or country estates have been built on many of the islands. The outer islands of the Archipelago, in the high sea, form the part most affected by erosion of wind and water, and are the most difficult of access. Wilder and more deserted, these form a veritable paradise for sailors. Many of the restaurants here, moreover, feature charac-

Utö.

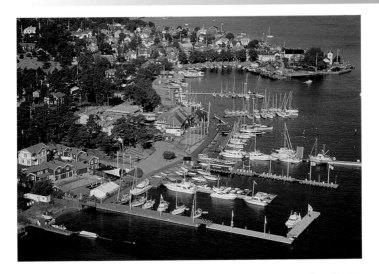

Sandhamn.

teristic dishes from the islands' cuisine, rich in the "flavour of the Archipelago".

Boats to the Archipelago depart from the Blasieholmen dock, opposite the Grand Hotel.

A fascinating excursion is a visit to the island of **Utö**, in the southern part of the Archipelago. Utö, with is sandy beaches and rocks, can be explored by bicycle. Iron began to be extracted here as early as the 12th century, and the island boasts Sweden's oldest iron mine, whilst the 18th-century miners' houses were later converted into summer residences. Visitors wishing to spend the night on the island will no doubt find lodgings in one of these houses. Many famous Swedish personalities have lived on Utö, including the dramatist August Strindberg and the painter Anders Zorn. A little further off, in the outer part of the Archipelago in the Baltic, is **Sandhamn**, where there was once a customs post. This island, with a permanent population of just one hundred or so souls, is one of the most frequented in the Archipelago, even in the low season. Inland, the houses huddle together, separated by narrow streets. Along the docks stand lines of tiny wooden houses, formerly fishermen's dwellings, and all along the coast are moored visiting boats, as Sandhamn is the headquarters of the Royal Stockholm Yacht Club. The island restaurant, founded in the 17th century, is open all the year round. Sandhamn also offers visitors many beautiful beaches.

Vaxholm, situated around 40 kilometres northeast of Stockholm and considered the gateway to the Archipelago, is a visit not to be missed. In summer, the island is transformed by the arrival of flocks of summer residents and tourists, and the boat journey to Vaxholm provides a splendid vision of the landscape of the inner core of the Archipelago, with its wooded islets and narrow straits. Vaxholm itself began to become fashionable in the second half of the 19th century, when it became the custom to spend the summer by the sea.

The island continues to be visited by Swedes and visitors alike, who sail here by yacht to eat herring at its restaurants or to enjoy a stroll around its picturesque wooden chalets, surrounded by leafy vegetation. It was prohibited to built stone houses on Sandhamn until 1912. A fort was built on the island during the reign of Gustav Vasa, and this has now been converted into a museum. Vaxholm played an important role in the defence of the coast, safeguarding access to Stockholm from the sea. It was precisely at Vaxholm that the Danish forces led by Christian II entered Swedish waters to conquer the capital.

Boats for Vaxholm leave from the Blasieholmen dock, near the National Museum. The island can also be reached by bus from Östra Station.

Millesgården

Another suggested excursion, of interest not only to art-lovers, is a visit to the Millesgården sculpture museum and park on Lidingö

Boats to Vaxholm depart from the dock by the National Museum.

Vaxholm: the fort.

island, east of Stockholm. Millesgården was established by the sculptor Carl Milles and his wife, the painter Emma Lundberg, and was originally the couple's studio and home. Milles invested much of the fortune he had made from the sale of his sculptures in the estate, building great staircases and terraces to install his works, creating an ideal environment for them, a peculiar mixture

Millesgården.

Two views of Millesgården.

of architecture, sculpture, nature and water. Some of the columns which adorn the gardens were rescued by Milles from old buildings, from the original Drama Theatre and from the opera house of Gustav III. This site, with its buildings, staircases and gardens, occupies a total area of some 18,000 m².

Milles' sculptures, some examples of which we have already seen in the city itself –"Orpheus" in

the Hötorget Concert House, or "Gustav Vasa", at the entrance to the Nordic Museum– are imbued with a lightness which creates the illusion that they are floating in the air, flying. Millesgården also possesses a fine collection of Greek and Roman works, as well as French and Italian paintings. In the music room is an organ from Salzburg which, it is said, Mozart's father used to play.

Boats depart for the island from the Nybrokajen and Strömkajen docks in Blasieholmen. Alternatively, visitors can take the underground to Ropsten station, where they can catch a bus to Millesgården.

Hagaparken, Bergianska Trädgardet, National Natural History Museum and Ulriksdal Palace

Another recommended visit, not far from the city centre, is to the first urban national park in the world, **Hagaparken**. Created in the late-18th century at the command of Gustav III in English

The Koppartälten, or the Copper Marques, in Hagaparken.

style, the park is adorned with pavilions, temples and other architectural elements. At the north end are the **Koppartälten** (Copper Marquees), which have the appearance of a Roman military tent and were used to billet the royal guard. A small museum is installed in one of the marquees, and it was originally planned to build a great palace here, with a National Museum, but this idea was abandoned on the death of Gustav III.

Near to the marquees is the **Fjärilhuset**, where hundreds of butterflies flit amongst tropical plants, and where there is also a winter garden where birds fly in "limited freedom". The present king, Carl Gustav, spent his childhood in the modest **Haga slott** palace, which is now used to provide accommodation for official guests.

Fjärilhuset.

83

Ulriksdals slott.

Near to the waterside is the **Gustav III pavilion** and, beside it, the **Ekotemplet**, which resembles a Greek temple and was used as an auxiliary dining-room in the summer months. The Gustav III:s pavilion is a small palace with an unassuming exterior which is, however, the most beautiful building in the entire park, designed in collaboration with the king himself, who planned to fix his residence here, though he died before he could fulfil his wish. The walls of the interior are decorated using a special painting technique which creates the illusion of niches and columns, whilst the salon is adorned with Pompeii-style frescoes. One of the most attractive rooms of all is the Mirror Room, with its air of force and serene beauty.

Other places of interest near Hagaparken include, three kilometres to the north, on the banks of Lake Edsviken, the baroque palace of **Ulriksdal** and, on the other side of Lake Brunnsviken, the **Bergianska Trädgardet** botanical gardens and the **Naturhistoriska riksmuseet (National Natural History Museum)**, one of the finest museums of its type in the world. The museum's facilities also include the Cosmonova, the most modern planetarium in Sweden, where films are shown on an Omnimax screen.

Cosmonova, in the Natural History Museum.

Dalahäst, the little red wooden horse which has become a symbol of Sweden.

ARTS AND CRAFTS

Swedish arts, crafts and design are known the whole world over, for Sweden has wisely kept alive its old traditions, combining them with new ideas and fashions. The centre for glasswork is in Småland, in the southwest of the country, where such famed factories as Orrefors and Kosta-Boda have their factories. Orrefors, founded in 1898, became world famous in the 1920s. The two companies, which merged some years ago, present new collections every year, as well as producing limited editions of from one to sixty pieces, signed by their designer. The glassworks currently has a team of ten designers devoted to the creation of the finest glass products.

Dalarna province, famous for its woodcraft products, hand-painted and brightly-coloured, is where the little red horse (Dalahäst), which has become a symbol of Sweden, is produced. The woodcutters of the region used to amuse themselves after a long day's work by sitting around the fire carving wooden toys. The horse was not only an important part of everyday life, but also held a special place in Scandinavian mythology, as Odin, the father of the gods, possessed an eight-footed horse, Sleipner. However, it was in 1939 that the image of the horse acquired fame and relevance in modern times, with the construction of a giant horse from Dalarna, installed at the entrance to the Swedish pavilion at the Exhibition in New York.

ARTS AND CRAFTS

The arts and crafts of the Lapps, which form an ethnic minority group in the north of the country, include articles in stone, wood, tin, reindeer bone and leather. Finally, Swedish design –industrially-produced everyday utensils– is widely appreciated due to its characteristic purity of style and functionality.

Glasswork.

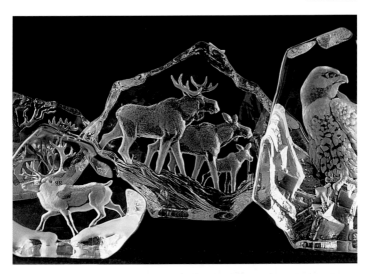

Mustard Baltic herring

Gut approx. 1kg Baltic herring. Whisk 2 egg yolks, 2dl whipping cream and a heaped tbsp of sweet mustard together. Marinate the herring in the marinade for a few minutes. Coat the fish in seasoned breadcrumbs and fry in a generous amount of butter. Serve with mashed potato and parsley butter. Serves 4.

Marinated salmon

Fillet the middle portion of a fresh (frozen) salmon and remove any remaining bones. Moisten with a little oil. Marinate the fillets, flesh sides together, for 20-24 hours in a mixture of 1 part sugar, 1 part salt, crushed white pepper grains and a generous amount of chopped dill. During this time, slight pressure should be applied. Cut into slices and serve with a mustard sauce. To make sauce, mix together tbsp mild mustard, 1 tsp French mustard, 1 dessertspoon sugar and 1.5 tbsps vinegar. Finally, add approx. 2dl cooking oil (not olive oil) drop by drop and chopped dill.

Swedish Pyttipanna

Brown equal amounts of diced onion, diced potato and diced meat, sausage and ham leftovers separately in butter. Mix together. Serve with fried egg, pickled beetroot and pickled gherkin and tomato ketchup or brown sauce.

Jansson's Temptation

5-6 potatoes, 1-2 onions, 150g anchovy fillets, 1 tbsp butter, 2dl double cream.

Cut potatoes into thin strips. Slice onion and fry lightly. Line casserole with alternate layers of potato, onion and anchovies. End with a top layer of potato. Add a few dabs of butter and the juice from the anchovies. Bake for 30 minutes. Mix in the cream and bake for a further 15 minutes. Serves 4.

TOURIST INFORMATION

Stockholm Visitors Board AB

Stockholm Visitors Board AB (SVB) is the official convention and visitors bureau of Stockholm and fully owned by the City of Stockholm. SVB runs the tourist office Stockholm Tourist Centre and the interactive information station Stockholms-panelen www.stockholmtown.com

Stockholm Tourist Centre

The new Stockholm Tourist Centre gives a foretaste of the pulsating city of Stockholm. The office helps you with accommodation and sights. Additionally, the office sells tickets to events, sightseeing tours, maps, and books as well as the Stockholm Card.
Visit: Stockholm Tourist Centre, Sweden House, Hamngatan 27, entrance Kungsträdgården.
Contact: ph: +46 8 508 285 08, Fax: +46 8 508 285 09,
e-mail: info@svb.stockholm.se
Opening Hours:
- Monday – Friday: 9 am – 7 pm
- Saturday: 10 am – 5 pm
- Sunday: 10 am – 4 pm
- Closed: Dec 24, 25 and Jan 1

Book your accommodation

Book your hotel room directly on the web at www.stockholmtown.com/hotels or visit Stockholm Tourist Centre.

Guide booking

Stockholm Visitors Board assists with reservations of licensed Stockholm guides, archipelago guides and licensed taxi guides. We work with more than 400 guides who together master around 30 languages. Telephone hours: Mon to Fri 9 am – 5 pm. Tel: +46 8 508 285 08, Fax: +46 8 508 285 12, e-mail: guides@svb.stockholm.se, www.stockholmtown.com

The Stockholm Card

The Stockholm Card is amazingly extensive, offering, in addition to everything else, a thorough selection of the best that Stockholm has to offer in terms of attractions and sights. The Stockholm Card gives you free entry to 75 museums and attractions, free travel by public transport, free sightseeing by boat as well as several other bonus offers. You decide whether you want a card that is valid for 24, 48 or 72 hours. Buy it online on: www.stockholmtown.com/stockholmcard or at the Stockholm Tourist Centre.

EMERGENCIES:
The free emergency telephone number for **Ambulance, Police or Fire Brigade** is 112 from all public telephones in Sweden. The **city police** are courteous and always happy to help visitors. The general telephone number of the Stockholm Police is 401 00 00, and there are also district police stations in each neighbourhood and at Central Station.

CHEMIST'S SHOPS:
Medicines for many ailments not requiring doctor's prescription can be obtained from chemist's shops in the city. C. W. Scheele, near Central Station, is an all-night chemist's open all the year round.

ALCOHOL:
Swedish law restricts the sale of alcoholic drinks, beer and win, which can only be purchased at branches of the state monopoly shop, Systembolaget. Infringements of drinking and driving laws are severely punished.

POST OFFICE:
There are local post offices in all neighbourhoods. Letterboxes in Sweden are blue for local mail and yellow for other destinations at home and abroad.

INTERNET CAFÉS:
- **Access IT.** Kulturhuset, Sergels Torg. Tel: 08-508 314 89.
- **Nine.** Odengatan 44. Tel: 08-612 99 19.
- **Sverigehuset.** Hamngatan 27.
- **Kulturhusets Internetcafé** (Internet surfing centre). Sergels Torg. Tel: 408 314 89.

PUBLIC TRANSPORT:
Stockholm's excellent public transport network provides access to the vast majority of places of tourist interest in and around the city. The underground has 100 stations on three main lines (red, yellow and blue) which converge at the central metro station, T-centralen. This, in turn, connects with the railway station, with national, international and local train departures, and bus lines.

An easy and economical way of seeing the city is to use the city bus network. The purchase of two coupons allows visitors to travel for the two subsequent hours. The most attractive bus routes are those of the number 3, 4, 46, 47, 62 and 69, which go around much of the central part of Stockholm, with stops near many tourist attractions. Services generally run on time, and fares vary by route and destination.

ATTRACTIONS FOR CHILDREN:

Stockholm is very much a child-friendly city. Most of the favourite attractions for younger visitors are found in the Djurgården area, such as **Junibacken**, where children can see characters and scenes from the world of the Swedish writer Astrid Lindgren, as well as other characters from Swedish children's literature, the **Vasa** Museum, the **Gröna Lund funfair** and the **Skansen Open-Air Museum**.

Right in the heart of the city, the **House of Culture (Kulturhuset)** offers a variety of cultural activities for children whilst, in the out-skirts of Stockholm is the interesting and educational **National Natural History Museum (Naturhistoriska Riksmuseet)**, whose facilities include the **Cosmonova**, Sweden's most modern plan-etarium, which shows films about the cosmos on a great Omnimax screen, the largest format in existence today. The use of the latest technology has a powerful impact on spectators, who feel irresistibly drawn into the spectacle they are viewing.

OUTDOOR ACTIVITIES:
Stockholm, a city surrounded by water and with many parks, is ideal for the practice of an infinity of activities in the open air, which are an important component in the Swedish way of life. The city offers a range of different pursuits at each changing season of the year. In spring, summer and autumn, its magnificent golf courses, jogging tracks and cycle circuits are a delight, whilst the crystal-clear water, even in the very centre of the city, is an invitation to take a dip on hot summer days.

GOLF:
There are some 80 golf courses within easy range of the city centre.
- **Djursholms Golfklubb**. Hagbardsvägen, Djursholm. Tel: 544 964 51. A popular course. Visitors are advised to book in advance.
- **Ullna Golf**. Rosenkälla Åkersberga. Tel: 514 412 30.
- **Drottningsholms golfklubb**. Drottningholm. Tel: 759 00 85.

TENNIS:
There are outdoor tennis courts all over the city.
- **Kungliga Tenishallen.** Lidingövägen. Tel: 664 38 88. With open-air courts. The venue of the Stockholm Open international tournament each November.

BATHING:
There are several heated open-air swimming-pools relatively near to the city centre for visitors in summer.

Open-air swimming-pools:
- **Eriksdalsbadet.** Hammarby slussv. 8. Tel: 508 402 50.
- **Kampementsbadet** (22 June - 22 August). Sandhamnsgatan, Gärdet. Tel: 661 62 16.
- **Vanadisbadet** (22 June - 22 August). Vanadislunden. Tel: 34 33 00.

WATER SPORTS:
Visitors can hire canoes, rowing boats and pedal boats, as well as motor boats for longer trips, near Djurgården bridge, Djurgårdsbron.

BALLOON TRIPS:
Visitors can enjoy a bird's-eye panoramic view of the city by taking a balloon trip over the roofs of Stockholm.
- **Ballongfirman Far & Flyg**. Gröndalsvägen 80. Tel: 645 77 00.

PLACES OF INTEREST, MUSEUMS, ART GALLERIES AND CASTLES IN STOCKHOLM:

Aquaria vattenmuseum/Aquaria Water Museum
Scandinavian and tropical watery environments, with sharks and other fish, corals and waterfalls with salmon and trout. Falkenbergsgatan, 2. Tel: 660 49 40.

Arkitekturmuseet/Swedish Museum of Architecture
1000 years of Swedish architectural and building history. Exercisplan. Tel: 587 270 00.

Armémuseum/Royal Army Museum
1000 years of military history, illustrating the development of the armed forces and society. Exhibitions featuring full-scale reproductions. Riddargatan 13. Tel: 788 95 60.

Bergianska Trädgården/Bergianska Gardens
Botanical gardens with over 9,000 species of plants with two greenhouses to keep the area green all the year round. Five kilometres north of Stockholm. Tel: 545 917 00.

Biologiska museet/Museum of Biology
Scandinavian animal life seen in natural surroundings. Lejonslätten. Tel: 442 82 15.

Cosmonova
Film showings in the largest-format screen in the world. Five kilometres north of Stockholm. Tel: 519 531 30.

Drottningholmsslott/Drottningholm Castle
Residence of the royal family. The visit includes the Castle Theatre (Slottsteater) and the Theatre Museum (Teatermuseum). Ten kilometres east of Stockholm. Tel: 402 62 80.

Historiska museet/History Museum
Devoted to prehistoric and Viking times and the Middle Ages, and featuring the magnificent Gold Room, which contains many invaluable finds and treasures. Narvavägen 13-17. Tel: 519 556 00.

Junibacken
A space devoted to children's culture. Galärvarvsvägen. Tel: 587 230 00.

Kaknästornet/Kaknäs Tower
The kaknästower is 155 m (480 feet) high, and the highest building in Scandinavia. From the top of the tower there is a wonderful panorama view over the city. Ladugårdsgärdet, Touristinfo. Tel: 667 21 05.

Kulturhuset/The House of Culture
A centre devoted to photography, multimedia art, fashion, music, dance and the theatre. Sergels Torg 3. Tel: 508 315 08.

Kungliga Slottet/Royal Palace
The king's official residence. Besides various rooms, the Palace Museum and the Gustav III Museum of Antiquities are open to the public. Gamla stan. Tel: 402 61 30.

Leksaksmuseet/Toy Museum
A five-storey building which houses thousands of toys. Mariatorget 1. Tel: 641 61 00.

Liljevalchs konsthall/Liljevalchs Art Gallery
One of the most beautiful exhibition centres in northern Europe. Shows featuring the Swedish, Scandinavian and international art of the last few centuries. Djurgårdsvägen 60. Tel: 508 313 30.

Livrustkammaren/Royal Armoury
Slottsbacken 3, by the Royal Palace. Tel: 519 555 50.

Medeltidsmuseet/ Museum of Medieval Stockholm
Stockholm in medieval times. Strömparterren, Norrbro. Tel: 508 317 90.

Millesgården
A park containing sculptures and the house and studio of sculptor Carl Milles. Herserudsvägen 30, Lidingö. Tel: 446 75 90.

Moderna Museet/Museum of Modern Art
A collection of contemporary Swedish and international art. Exercisplan. Tel: 519 552 82.

Nationalmuseum/National Museum
Sweden's largest art museum. Södra Blasieholmshamnen. Tel: 519 543 00.

Naturhistoriska riksmuseet/National Natural History Museum
One of the finest in the world of its type. The facilities here also include Cosmonova. Five kilometres north of Stockholm. Tel: 519 540 00.

Nordiska museet/Nordic Museum
The traditions of the Swedish people from the mid-16th century to the present day. Djurgårdsvägen 6-16. Tel: 519 560 00.

Östasiatiska museet/Museum of Far Eastern Art
The largest collection of Asian art in Europe. Tyghusplan. Tel: 519 557 70.

Sjöhistoriska museet/Museum of Maritime History
The most important museum devoted to merchant navigation, naval defence and shipbuilding. Djurgårdsbrunnsvägen 24. Tel: 519 549 00.

Skansen
Open-air museum, zoo and park. Djurgårdsslätten 49. Tel: 442 80 00.

Stockholms Stadsmuseum/Stockholm City Museum
This history of the city and its inhabitants from the 16th century to the present. Ryssgården. Tel: 508 316 00.

Tekniska museet/Museum of Science and Technology
Exhibits relating to the history of technology and industry in Sweden. Museivägen 7. Tel: 450 56 00.

Thielska galleriet/Thielska Gallery
Featuring an important collection of Nordic art. Sjötullsbacken 6-8. Tel: 662 58 84.

Ulriksdals Slott/Ulriksdal Castle
Furnishings and decoration of outstanding historical interest. Seven kilometres north of Stockholm. Tel: 402 61 30.

Waldemarsudde (Prins Eugens)/Prince Eugen's Palace
Art collection, gardens and park. Prins Eugens väg, 6. Tel: 545 837 00.

Vasamuseet/Vasa Museum
Featuring the ship of the same name, which sank on its maiden voyage in 1628. Galärvarvet. Tel: 519 548 00.

CONTENTS

EDITORIAL FISA ESCUDO DE ORO, S.A.
Veneçuela, 105 - 08019 Barcelona
Tel: 93 230 86 00 - www.eoro.com

I.S.B.N. 978-91-972076-1-4
Printed in Spain
Legal Dep. B. 29384-2008